Abuse
to
Favor

Jo Ann Aleman
Sharon Kay Ball

The Freedom Series
Created by Michelle Borquez

AspirePress

Torrance, California

Abuse to Favor

© Copyright 2013 God Crazy/Bella Publishing
Aspire Press, a division of Rose Publishing, Inc.
4733 Torrance Blvd., #259
Torrance, California 90503 USA
www.aspirepress.com

Register your book at www.aspirepress.com/register
Get inspiration via email, sign up at www.aspirepress.com

The views and opinions expressed in this book are those of the authors and do not necessarily express the views of Aspire Press, nor is this book intended to be a substitute for mental health treatment or professional counseling.

Printed in the United States.

Contents

The Authors

Jo Ann Aleman grew up in a violently abusive home. Despite promises to herself to break the cycle of abuse, she found herself seeking out relationships that continued that abuse—until she discovered the truth of God's Word and his will for her life.

Sharon Kay Ball is a licensed professional counselor and a mother to three children. In addition to her private practice, Sharon is a staff counselor at her church. Her own personal experience with suffering, the daily grind of single parenting, and counseling her clients has given Sharon tremendous compassion and insight for those dealing with life's tragedies and trials.

Chapter 1

Jo Ann's Story

By Jo Ann Aleman

"When we are no longer able to change a situation, we are challenged to change ourselves."—Viktor Frankl

As children we dream about who we want to be, what we want to have, and how we will live our lives when we grow up. For me, my dreams were shaped out of a childhood that was fenced in by fear. Although abuse was my family's "normal" and my momma's "normal," my little heart knew it wasn't normal at all. Even though we are all somewhat conditioned by our environment, something deep inside of us reveals the truth. I knew that the things my little eyes saw at home were not what most kids were exposed to in their homes.

There were many nights I would lie awake uttering what I believed were prayers to God for change, only to discover later in life that I had actually been making commitments or promises to myself: *I will never live like this when I grow up. I will never let a man treat me this way. I will never depend on anyone else to take care of me.* I settled in my heart that I would be different. Yet my heart cried out for someone to sweep in and rescue me from all that I knew. The image I had of the perfect life did not include abuse of any kind. I would find my Prince Charming, someone who would love me and love the Lord, someone who would protect me and never hurt me or the family we would have. Little did I know that what I truly needed was not Prince Charming, but the King of Kings. It would take many years of heartache before I would finally leave abuse behind and realize that I have the favor of my true Savior.

Although my father was loving to his children and an incredible provider, he was also, at times, very abusive to my mom. Consequently, our weekends consisted of fear. Our home life changed drastically as the weekend approached. My father never came straight home after work on Friday nights. He would stop at the local bar to shoot a few games of pool and drink until he could barely drive. Once he arrived home, our hearts would pound with fear as the screaming and abuse would begin. As soon as he passed out, my mom had us quickly gather our clothes—just enough for the night—and we would escape the environment of rage before my father woke up. My childhood involved us leaving our home most weekends, sometimes for a few days, sometimes much longer. My mother always intended to leave my father for good, but with five children, she found imposing on her family members hard. In an attempt for some normalcy while away, she would enroll us in a new school, only to withdraw us and go back home when my father promised once again that life would be better. Unfortunately, the abusive cycle of chaos would continue for many years.

Our hearts would pound with fear.

In spite of her being abused, my mother was determined to keep her family intact. She was faithful to her own childhood commitments. As a little girl, my sweet momma had uttered prayers of her own, not realizing that those prayers were promises born out of her own abusive childhood. My mother suffered greatly at the hands of a very cruel stepfather who physically, mentally, and emotionally abused her and her siblings until they became old enough to stand up for themselves. She had promised herself that she would never allow her children to grow up with a stepfather, so she kept her marriage vows to my daddy and remained in the home. We didn't have a stepfather, yet she did not escape the pattern of abuse that had been set for her.

My image of how a man treats a woman and how a woman responds to that treatment was formed by what I saw in my parents. I didn't like it, and my heart knew something was wrong, but abuse was my "normal." Despite my childhood dreams, the abuse set the stage for me to be destined for heartache. Many times we think of abuse as being only physical; however, abuse takes on many forms. Sexual abuse, verbal abuse, and emotional abuse—even neglect—are all perversions of real, unconditional love. But they are sometimes hard to recognize. The victim of abuse is inclined to excuse the abuser because of love for the abuser. A child, even one not being physically abused, is still scarred by the experience of watching a loved one being abused. Although it would take years to surface, for me the damage had been done.

When I grew up and started searching for my Prince Charming, the lasting effects of my parents' abuse cycle would take center stage in my own life. Without thinking about the consequences, I married for the first time at the tender age of seventeen. We were very young and from very different cultures. But everything appeared to be just as I had always pictured it in my dreams: a man who loved me, who loved God, and a family who was involved in ministry. Alas, this perfect equation included me! I was free on the surface, yet broken and deeply wounded inside. I so desperately longed for someone to rescue me that I jumped on the first train to freedom.

Soon into our marriage, I began to see a very different man surface. Although I knew this was not the "happily ever after" I had pictured, in just six months time, I became pregnant. Little Chelsi Marie Gentry brought hope for a short while to an already shaky foundation. I did not want to expose my daughter to a stepfather, so I tried to make my marriage work. Sadly, not long after I had my daughter, I became very ill and spent the next two years in and out of hospitals. Eventually I had to have a hysterectomy, taking away my chances of bearing any more children. I was barely into my twenties and felt like even less of a woman. I felt worthless. My marriage faltered, and after four short years, we divorced.

There were many things that led to the failure of my first marriage. Our young age, our different cultural backgrounds, and family difficulties were all factors ... and then there was the abuse. Even though I was not being abused in the same manner as my mother had been, my husband's words were degrading and at times he was physical. In spite of the heartbreaking reality of feeling like a failure, I could no longer stay in the marriage. I still longed for love—for the perfect marriage and family—but I had absolutely no idea how to find, create, or sustain what my heart desired.

Nonetheless, that didn't stop me from forging ahead. Just thirty days after my divorce was final, I made the decision to get married again. Maybe I didn't know how to be on my own. Maybe I was afraid to go home. Whatever the root cause, at just twenty-one years old, I married a man ten years my senior. This time, I was determined to make it work—determined not to fail.

He was bent on complete destruction.

The next six years sent me spiraling into a life of abuse much like the childhood home I had left. Not only did I endure physical abuse, but also emotional abuse. My husband refused to work and was always out. Many nights I was awakened by his fists pummeling my face. He would get so drunk that he would black out, and the next morning we would wake up to a house that looked like a tornado had ripped through it: broken pictures on the floor, plants overturned, and holes in the walls. He was bent on complete destruction. Sometimes I would come home from a night of sleeping in my car at the park to find everything destroyed; then I'd spend the next several hours cleaning it all up. It was a vicious cycle that I couldn't break. My heart was not prepared to admit that I had made another mistake.

My parents lived across the street, and by this time my father was a changed man. He was no longer abusive. Still, I never ran home for safety. I couldn't bear to break my parents' hearts. During those years, my daughter spent more time in my parents' home than she did in mine. It broke my heart, but I knew that if she was in their home, she was in a safe place. I financially supported my husband and endured his abuse for six years before he decided he no longer wanted to be married. He packed my daughter's and my belongings, set them out on the front yard, and told me to get out of his house. Devastated by the fact that I had failed once again at the one thing I wanted most in life, I filed for divorce for the second time.

Still, my childhood dream of the life I longed to have continued to tug at my heart, and I jumped right into the arms of another man in my search for love. I needed to feel worthy. My actions, however, were foolish and completely selfish; and I blindly fell into a trap without thinking about how what I was doing would affect my daughter. After only a few weeks of knowing him, my daughter and I moved in with the man who would become husband number three. He was a widower with a seven-year-old daughter, and his life was as broken as mine. After several months of living together, we decided to get married. Little did I know that the next twelve years of my life would center on intimidation and fear, but this time, it would also directly include my daughter.

Within a year of marrying, I rededicated my life to God, but I was still broken. What I needed was not a savior but *the* Savior. I knew about Jesus. I even thought I had a relationship with him, but I never understood my value to him. Religion, not real relationship, guided my decisions. So when the abuse cycle began again, I felt that I could not leave my third marriage. I had made marriage vows before God; I could not break them again. In his brokenness, my husband lashed out physically, emotionally, sexually, and verbally. His words had a way of cutting me to the core. I already felt like a failure. I already felt worthless. His words only confirmed my feelings. They shaped me, took root in my heart, and I believed the things he said. His venomous phrases echoed in my heart: "You will never amount to anything."

"You're a mutt."

"No one will ever want you."

> My heart [was] shattered and scarred.

For over a decade, I lived on a roller coaster of abuse. Not only was my

15

heart shattered and scarred, but also my body now bore the visible scars of physical abuse. In addition, my daughter suffered a great deal of emotional abuse. My husband was jealous of my daughter, and when I traveled for work, he often deprived her of things—food, money, television, and much more. He called her names and would force her to sit in a corner while he and his daughter watched television. She rebelled, falling into relationships that were abusive, experimenting with drugs, and indulging in any other form of escape she could find. But if I gave up on my marriage, I felt I would be letting down the Lord. So I stayed. But eventually the marriage still ended. I found myself once again broken and alone.

After my third divorce, I determined to find healing. Some people might think that being made whole takes place in an instant. One good cry at an altar and behold, all things are new. The truth is that the healing process is just that—a process. Don't get me wrong; I believe God's Word is true: "If anyone is in Christ, the new creation has come: The old has gone, the new is here!" (2 Corinthians 5:17). However this passage speaks of reconciliation, not instant healing. My healing process has been ongoing over the past eight years.

I have had many victories in my life and know that I have overcome abuse. I have grown in the realization that I am not responsible for the decisions and abuse caused by others. I have found freedom from being the "responsible" one. I recognize that there is only One who can truly change the heart of a person. I only have to surrender to God. He alone brings healing, restoration, and new life. I now feel as if everywhere I go, God's shield of favor follows me. During the past eight years, I have earned both a bachelor's and a master's degree. I don't boast about such accomplishments because they were mine, but I revel in the goodness of God for surrounding me with grace, not only to set goals, but also to meet them.

Because of God's Word, I am able to see myself in a different light that has forever changed my life. After my third divorce, I purposed in my heart to dive into God's Word and better understand his will for my life.

God gave me clarity.

God gave me clarity and has revealed the truth that I am his, and I have been created in his image—beautiful. He became my provision, my sustainer, and my anchor. With his help, I was able to rebuild my relationship with my daughter. Today we are closer than we ever were. She is now a beautiful wife and the mother of four adorable children, working out her own healing. Our lives have come together, and we believe that God has paved the path for our futures—the futures he intends for us.

I know that I have God's favor. God has opened doors for me and for my daughter "that no one can shut" (Revelation 3:8). He is better than Prince Charming. I am the beloved daughter of the King of Kings. His Word has given me newfound hope. My failures and brokenness have led me to the cross. They forced me to face my childhood and my fears. I have chosen to believe in him and to believe the words he has spoken about me. His Word has revealed his promises, his view of me, and his plans for me. There is freedom in surrender, and I have surrendered all to him. In doing so, God has granted me life and favor. He has preserved my spirit.

> "You have granted me life and lovingkindness; and Your care has preserved my spirit."
> —Job 10:12 (NASB)

Abuse to Favor

Chapter 2

Bible Study

By Sharon Kay Ball

"Silence in the face of evil is itself evil:
God will not hold us guiltless. Not to speak
is to speak. Not to act is to act."
— Dietrich Bonhoeffer

Whatever the relationship may be—pastor to parishioner, father to daughter, boss to employee, older sibling to younger sibling, teacher to student, husband to wife, boyfriend to girlfriend, or friend to friend—the strategy behind abuse is simple: to maintain power and control over the victim. Good leaders will not abuse their power of authority. When there is a natural inequality of power because of the nature of the relationship, like a teacher to a student, a good teacher will always respect that authority, not abuse it to gain more power over the student.

In Jo Ann's story, you can see the pattern of domestic abuse: husband to wife and father to children. Jo Ann's father abused the authority that was given to him as husband and father within the family household. This power was used to control the members of the family through intimidation tactics, poisonous words, and physical strength, trapping them in a vicious cycle of abuse.

Conflict in relationships is normal, and sometimes, in the heat of the moment, one person might yell, make a smart remark, or belittle the other. But the line between normal conflict and abuse is crossed when you see these "moments" become patterns fueled by power that leaves one partner consistently dominating the other.

God is not silent on the issue of abuse. In fact, the Bible has a lot to say about it. As you go through this study, you'll discover that—as one of the Old Testament prophets wrote long ago—"the LORD ... is a mighty savior. He will take delight in you with gladness. With his love, he will calm all your fears" (Zephaniah 3:17 NLT).

A Story of Abuse in the Bible

The story of Saul and David in the Old Testament is one of the clearest biblical examples of abuse. Although the abuse occurs male to male, the abuse pattern mirrors domestic abuse. Abuse crosses all gender, cultural, religious, age, and ethnic boundaries.

The story of Saul and David in 1 Samuel 16–27 shows us:

- A vivid picture of the abuse cycle

- A portrait of the abuser, King Saul, and the victim, David

↠ A biblical example of addressing abuse, finding safety, and forgiving your abuser

Let's begin by setting the stage in 1 Samuel 16–18. The young David takes up employment in King Saul's household by playing the harp for the king whenever the king becomes tormented by his thoughts. (The Spirit of the Lord had departed from Saul; see 1 Samuel 16:14.)

When war breaks out between the Philistines and Israel, David courageously goes out and slays the giant Goliath on the battlefield. King Saul is impressed with David's triumph over Goliath, and from that day forward he did not let David return home. David and Saul's son Jonathan quickly become kindred spirits.

King Saul becomes jealous of David when the people praise David more than Saul. So Saul decides to keep "a close eye" on David (1 Samuel 18:9).

What signs have you picked up on so far that suggest that this relationship could become abusive?

_____

_____

_____

_____

_____

_____

_____

As the story unfolds, David continues to find favor with the Lord and the people, which causes Saul to become even more angry. During one of David's times playing the harp for the king, Saul tries to kill David with a spear. When that doesn't work, he secretly tries to have David killed twice by sending him to war. Then he offers David his daughter Michal as a wife if David kills a certain number of enemy Philistines. Saul hopes David will be killed in battle; that way no one would know that he had been behind David's death. But when David succeeds, Saul becomes more afraid of David. When he learns that his daughter Michal really loves David, Saul's fear and anger increase even further. So King Saul turns to Jonathan, one of his sons and David's best friend. He orders Jonathan and his servants to kill David.

List some character traits you see in King Saul.

_____

_____

_____

_____

_____

_____

List some character traits you see in David.

_____

_____

_____

_____

_____

_____

_____

In 1 Samuel 19, Jonathan warns David of his father's plan, and David flees. Jonathan then pleads with his father on behalf of David. When Saul promises not to hurt David, David returns to the household. This is good news because King Saul has recognized his problem and changed, right? No. David is once again playing the harp for Saul, and Saul gets angry and throws another spear at David!

David flees to his home where he and his wife Michal develop and execute a plan for his safe escape. When Saul's army arrives to kill David, they discover that he is not there.

From Jo Ann's Story

"I lived on a roller coaster of abuse."

What patterns of domestic abuse do you see emerging in this story?

_____

_____

_____

_____

_____

_____

At this point in the story, David is now separated from his friends and family in order to preserve his life. But he is able to meet secretly with Jonathan and explain how distraught he is trying to figure out what he has done so wrong that has made King Saul so angry—angry enough to seek out his death (1 Samuel 20).

Jonathan still believes that his father will not hurt David, so he and David come up with a plan to test whether or not Saul has truly changed. If Saul has changed, Jonathan will give David a signal that it is safe to come back to the palace. If Saul has not changed, Jonathan will signal David to flee and never return.

The plan is simple: David is not going to come to the New Moon feast at the palace, and Jonathan is going to let King Saul know that. But the news evokes such anger from Saul that while Jonathan explains David's absence, Saul verbally abuses Jonathan, calling him a "son of a perverse and rebellious woman!" and saying, "Don't I know that you have sided with [David]… to your own shame and to the shame of the mother who bore you?" (1 Samuel 20:30). *And get this:* King Saul hurls a spear at his own son! Jonathan runs to warn David to flee.

King Saul, however, is not going to give up trying to obliterate David. He has a thirst for power and control and until his thirst is quenched, he will continue his quest. In 1 Samuel 22, King Saul sends out an army to kill David. When they cannot find David, Saul orders the death of 85 priests and the entire community in which they had lived—men, women, *and* children! Why? Because they had helped David.

At this point in the story, what further character traits do you see in King Saul that mirror an abusive personality?

_____

_____

_____

_____

_____

How does David respond to King Saul's pursuit to destroy him?

_____

_____

_____

_____

_____

Do you think that it was a good idea for King Saul's daughter and son to devise plans to help David escape? Why or why not?

_____

_____

_____

_____

In 1 Samuel 24, David has the opportunity to kill King Saul while Saul is in a cave. David, however, chooses not to kill Saul and instead cuts off a piece of Saul's garment to prove to him that David had the chance to kill him. When David confronts Saul with this fact, Saul seeks forgiveness, weeps aloud, and begs for David to spare his family, because Saul knows that one day the Lord is going to make David king. David promises to spare Saul's family, and everyone goes about their business.

Time passes and David learns that King Saul is still plotting to kill him. David finds Saul at night, when he and his army are sleeping. David is under a tremendous amount of pressure from his men and advisors to kill King Saul, but David chooses not to exact revenge; he will not give way to such violence, because the king was anointed and David made an oath to spare him.

The next morning David makes the announcement that he could have killed Saul yet again. Saul says, "I have sinned. Come back, David my son. Because you considered my life precious today, I will not try to harm you again. Surely I have acted like a fool and have been terribly wrong" (verse 21). David forgives him, and each man then goes his own way.

But David realizes that King Saul is still obsessed with destroying him, so he decides to head to the land of the Philistines, hoping that Saul will finally stop pursuing him if he is out of Israel.

In the end, during battle with the Philistines, Saul, after being critically wounded, kills himself with his own sword.

Do you think King Saul values his word or promises? Why or why not?

_____

_____

_____

_____

_____

What in the story shows you that Saul has not changed his abusive pattern?

_____

_____

_____

_____

_____

Does David value the promises he makes to Saul? If so, how?

_____

_____

_____

_____

_____

_____

_____

_____

Do you think it was difficult for David to figure out if Saul had really changed? Why?

_____

_____

_____

_____

_____

The Cycle of Abuse

Take a good look at the domestic abuse cycle. Can you see phases of the cycle in the story of King Saul and David?

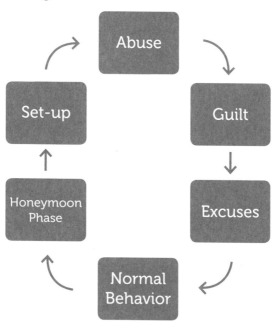

Abuse: David experiences King Saul's obsession, anger, and obvious attempts to kill David. In the beginning, however, David has a hard time figuring out why this person he loves is behaving this way.

Guilt: King Saul makes an oath on several occasions with his son, daughter, and David that he will not harm David again. He weeps and he begs for forgiveness.

Excuses: King Saul blames his irrational jealousy, anger, obsession, and hatred on David, because of David's favor from the Lord and from the people. It is David's fault.

Normal Behavior: After King Saul promises Jonathan, Michal, and David that he will not kill David, everyone goes their separate ways.

Honeymoon Phase: A period of calm takes place, allowing David and Jonathan to believe that David is safe.

Set-up: King Saul plans his next attack, and each attack escalates in violence.

Abuse: King Saul goes after David to kill him. Saul kills other people in his way.

Domestic abuse is on a continuum. It starts small, maybe with a push, then a slap, then a punch, then choking, and sometimes ends in death. It rarely stays with just the push.

Write down examples of how you've personally seen violence escalate. Can you see a pattern emerge?

_____

_____

_____

_____

_____

_____

_____

Let's take another look at the character traits of King Saul and David. Earlier you described some of their personality traits. Now let's list the traits that indicate that King Saul has an abusive personality:

Does not follow God: The spirit of the Lord is not with Saul.

Abuses his power of authority: Saul isolates David from his family. The relationship is king over commoner; elder man over younger man. Abusers like to keep their victims isolated from people who can help them.

Jealous and insecure: Saul is jealous of a boy!

Obsessive: Saul tries to destroy David again ... and again ... and again.

Full of rage: Not only does Saul try to kill David, but he even attempts to kill his own son Jonathan, and he does kill others who get in his way.

Revengeful and image-conscious, some might say narcissistic: Saul remains an enemy of David, although he knows the Lord is with David. He shows that he is religious on the outside, but inside he will not submit to God's authority.

Lies: Saul gives his word but does not keep it.

Lives in his own reality: Two of Saul's children (and probably all of his servants) see what is happening and try to reason with Saul that David has done nothing wrong, *but* Saul wants to see only his perception.

Creates "crazy-making" for the victim: A distraught David tries to figure out what he has done that justifies the punishment of death. He is confused. King Saul's tactic of keeping David "walking on eggshells" allows for the abuse to be unpredictable.

Verbally abusive: Saul berates his own son Jonathan.

Lacks empathy: Saul has no compassion for David. He even refuses to listen to his son and daughter as they try to reason with him.

Shifts blame: Saul justifies his behavior by saying it's David's fault.

Let's take a look at David's character traits:

Has a heart after God's heart: In speaking through the prophet Samuel, the Lord said, "But now your kingdom will not endure; the Lord has sought out a man after his own heart and appointed him ruler of his people, because you have not kept the Lord's command" (1 Samuel 13:14). Saul isn't concerned about God's heart or being obedient to what God desires. God was looking for someone who would follow after the things God desires. David has this heart.

Has God's favor: David doesn't have a perfect track record, so what excites God about David's heart and why does he find favor in him as the

Word tells us? God finds in David a man who keeps God's commandments. (You can see from the rest of the stories about David in the Bible that David doesn't always perform with perfect obedience to God. But when he is corrected and his attention is drawn to his sin, he always repents immediately. This shows that he guards and honors the command in his heart.)

Honest: David keeps his word consistently, even when under tremendous stress because his life is threatened.

Self-controlled: David has opportunities to kill his enemy, Saul, and he chooses not to.

Forgiving: David chooses to forgive Saul numerous times and leaves vengeance to the Lord.

Wise: David devises plans to ensure his safety.

Communicates well: David makes several attempts to reason and bargain with Saul to stop the abuse.

Patient: David never lets his anger get out of control.

The story of King Saul and David is powerful in understanding abusers and their victims. We see an abuser who is driven by power, intimidation, and a need to win at all costs. Because of this combination, he lives in his own reality; therefore, no one can help him unless he sees his own need for repentance. David eventually figures out that no matter what changes he makes in his own behavior, King Saul will not change his behavior. (This is important to note because abusers want their victims to take responsibility for *the abusers'* actions.) David begins to recognize the pattern of Saul's abusive control. He begins to see that Saul's abuse is fed by his desire to win at all costs. Saul views David as an enemy to wipe out. David knows this, so he escapes and finds safety.

Consider the following questions in light of what you've just learned from the story of Saul and David.

- What parts of the story of Saul and David mirror your own story?

- Is there an abuse cycle in one of your own relationships? If so, what does it look like?

- How have you seen yourself—or a family member or friend—trying to change in order to prevent another abusive attack?

- What is the difference between an occasional conflict in a relationship and a pattern of abuse?

- Is abuse caused by some aspect of your behavior? Your lack of submission? Or inability to communicate? Was abuse in David's story caused by David's behavior?

Take some time to journal your thoughts.

_____

_____

_____

_____

_____

_____

_____

_____

_____

_____

_____

_____

_____

_____

Abuse to Favor

Words that Destroy

Verbal and emotional abuse are patterns of behavior that are rooted in a desire to have power and control over someone, but can be delivered in craftier ways than physical abuse. This kind of abuse can be calculated to slowly destroy. It is a silent torture. Although this type of abuse does not leave physical scars, wounds are left upon the heart of the victim. It is a cruel form of abuse targeted at killing the victim's inner self through tactics that keep the victim under control.

From Jo Ann's Story

"His venomous phrases echoed in my heart."

Read the following definitions of each abusive strategy and see which ones resonate with you:

Rage: Yelling or displacing anger onto you. Sometimes there is no warning of when this rage will appear. It can arise over the smallest things. This is designed to keep you on your toes, unable to predict what's coming. It causes you to feel as if you can never rest as long as you are around this person, as if you must remain ever vigilant to protect yourself.

Silence: An obvious ignoring of your thoughts, ideas, concerns, and dreams in life.

Intimidation: This tactic is designed to create power through fear, actions, threats, or isolation.

Altering your sense of reality: Forcing a discussion and arguing far longer than is necessary to resolve a conflict, insisting that "what you thought" happened didn't really happen.

Criticizing: Finding fault in you in an adversarial way. It's not meant to build you up. It's delivered in such a way that it tears you down.

Blame-shifting: Blaming you for the injuries caused by the abuser, often making you feel as if you're going "crazy in the head." The abuser has a unique way of making you feel responsible for the abuser's behavior: If you had changed your behavior, then *he* would not have raged, hit, or called you a name. The abuser does not take responsibility for his actions; someone else is always to blame.

Which of these tactics have you experienced?

_____

_____

_____

_____

_____

_____

_____

How do you feel after you've been treated this way?

_____

_____

_____

_____

_____

How does each of these tactics give the abuser power and control?

_____

_____

_____

_____

_____

_____

Are you scared to tell someone about the verbal abuse you are going through? Does this fear keep you silent? Explain why.

_____

_____

_____

_____

_____

_____

_____

_____

_____

_____

_____

Take this verse to heart:

"For I am the Lord your God who takes hold
of your right hand and says to you, Do not
fear; I will help you."—Isaiah 41:13

Psalms and Proverbs are great places to start uncovering God's view of yelling, belittling, blaming, and intimidating:

"His mouth is full of lies and threats; trouble and evil are under his tongue."—Psalm 10:7

"You who practice deceit, your tongue plots destruction; it is like a sharpened razor."—Psalm 52:2

"The mouth of the righteous is a fountain of life, but the mouth of the wicked conceals violence."—Proverbs 10:11

"The words of the reckless pierce like swords, but the tongue of the wise brings healing."—Proverbs 12:18

"The tongue has the power of life and death, and those who love it will eat its fruit."
—Proverbs 18:21

"An angry person stirs up conflict, and a hot-tempered person commits many sins."
—Proverbs 29:22

Which verse resonates most with what you have gone through—or are going through now—in your relationships?

_____

_____

_____

_____

_____

What does Scripture say about how we are to treat each other verbally and emotionally?

_____

_____

_____

_____

_____

_____

Does Scripture allow us to pick and choose whom we want to treat well? Does it make an exception if the verbal and emotional abuse stays within in a family? *Not at all!* Why do you think God doesn't allow exceptions to these rules?

_____

_____

_____

_____

Have you allowed someone in your life to become the "exception to the rule"?

_____

_____

_____

_____

_____

_____

Is there a verse that you could memorize and use as a shield of protection during or after an attack of verbal or emotional abuse? Write it below.

_____

_____

_____

_____

Many times the abuser is known as a "really great guy" and most people "could never imagine him doing this." He typically is able to have control over his abuse, knowing exactly when and where to let his thirst for power come out. That power is targeted toward a weaker person and almost always done in private. Oftentimes, the victim will feel as if she is going crazy and wishes she had never been born. She stops dreaming about the future because her inner self has died. This is the epitome of living dead. Verbal and emotional abuse leave no physical marks, so the victim doesn't have any proof—even to herself—that the abuser has treated her in such an insidious way.

The author of the book of Ecclesiastes, whose character is known to be like that of wise King Solomon, understands this type of destitution. He says, "Again I looked and saw all the oppression that was taking place under the sun: I saw the tears of the oppressed—and they have no comforter; power was on the side of their oppressors—and they have no comforter. And I declared that the dead, who had already died, are happier than the living, who are still alive" (Ecclesiastes 4:1–2). The author understands that there are situations where oppressions and injustices in life may make a person wish that he or she had never been born or may make a person want to die.

This concept of a human being living in such oppression grieves the author. This is important to note because Ecclesiastes is considered one of the wisdom books, and the author is reviewing biblical wisdom versus worldly wisdom. He decides to include in his reflection of life that there are times when it may seem better to be dead than oppressed and alive.

How does this passage relate to the experience of verbal and emotional abuse?

_____

_____

_____

_____

_____

_____

_____

_____

_____

_____

Ecclesiastes 4:1–2 offers hope to the abuse victim. *How?* It affirms that there are injustices that are never heard by others, that victims go unnoticed and no one hears their cries. You are not alone if you have felt as if you're crazy. You are not alone if you have felt that things will never change. You are not alone if you have wished that you had not been born. The great author of Ecclesiastes knows this! If someone this wise recognizes the silent turmoil of a victim, then *maybe*:

- It is possible that you are *not* crazy!

- It is possible that you do *not* have the power to change certain things.

∾ And sometimes the pain is so agonizing that you would rather be dead than alive.

Does God see and hear the pain caused by domestic abuse? Does he hear the cries of those being wounded in secret? Yes, God hears and sees your pain and hurt. It does not go unnoticed.

Remember those beautiful songs in the book of Psalms? David wrote many of those about his experiences with heartache, abuse, and anger toward God. David endured abuse, so what he writes has credibility. David's psalms reflect perfectly his cry for help, his frustration with God's lack of response, and then his joy when he finally feels God's presence. David rides the roller coaster of emotions that life's trials bring, and he writes about all of them.

"Listen to me and answer me; I am worn out by my worries. I am terrified by the threats of my enemies, crushed by the

oppression of the wicked. They bring
trouble on me; they are angry with me and
hate me."— Psalm 55:2–3

In your Bible, look up and read **Psalm 5:2;
54:2; 61:1; 140:8–11; 142.** What do all these
verses have in common?

_____

_____

_____

_____

_____

_____

Can you relate to David's petition to God
during his seasons of desolation? If so, how?

_____

_____

_____

_____

_____

_____

_____

_____

_____

_____

Write your own psalm (song or poem). Share your petition with God; let him hear your heart and send you strength and deliverance.

_____

_____

_____

_____

_____

_____

_____

_____

_____

_____

_____

_____

_____

_____

From Jo Ann's Story

Getting Free!

In David's situation, he had to leave the house of Saul. He literally had to flee on several occasions to save his life. Yet it was hard for him to believe that Saul really wanted to kill him, and David even went back. This is a great example of how deceiving abusers can be with their behavior.

"God's shield of favor follows me."

Are you in a situation where your life is in danger and you need to leave? Read the directions at the end of this book and immediately develop your safe plan. It is very important to complete this process so that in the event you need to leave suddenly, you will know what to do.

Once you are safe and your abuser repents, you must wear the mantle of discernment like David did with King Saul. You must determine if your abuser truly has repented and changed his ways. A repentant heart recognizes personal sin, turns from it, and takes full responsibility for the sinful actions. Then new behaviors that are a clear reflection of God become the new patterns of interacting in the relationship. Remember, God sets the standard, not you. If true repentance has occurred, you will see consistent change over time (see Romans 8:5–9).

Four things you must know about abuse:

1. The abuse is *not about you! You* are *not* the reason for the chaos that you feel inside.

2. *You* cannot change your abuser, but you can change you.

3. *You* can take steps toward freedom, just like David did.

4. *Your* voice is heard by the greatest advocate to all victims: *God.* He understands how much pain your heart has felt; he gets it. This is e*mpowerment!* God is giving you the power to take back your life—your inner self.

The best part of taking back your life is that God, not you, is in charge of the punishment the abuser will receive. God gives you instructions on how to handle your deep desire for revenge:

"Do not take revenge, my dear friends, but leave room for God's wrath, for it is

written: 'It is mine to avenge; I will repay.'"
—Romans 12:19

"Do not repay evil with evil or insult with insult. On the contrary, repay evil with blessing, because to this you were called so that you may inherit a blessing."—1 Peter 3:9

"Never pay back evil with more evil. Do things in such a way that everyone can see you are honorable. Do all that you can to live in peace with everyone. Dear friends, never take revenge. Leave that to the righteous anger of God. For the Scriptures say, 'I will take revenge; I will pay them back,' says the LORD. Instead, 'If your enemies are hungry, feed them. If they are thirsty, give them something to drink. In doing this, you will heap burning coals of shame on their heads.' Don't let evil conquer you, but conquer evil by doing good."—Romans 12:17–21 (NLT)

God clearly says that he will take care of making sure the atrocities of life—including domestic abuse—are avenged. He will hand down the punishment.

If you believe that God hears your silent wounds and will avenge on your behalf and if you obey his command not to take matters into your own hands, you are free to focus on forgiving your abuser. God knows how hard this process is going to be, so he walks beside you, bearing the burden of vengeance so that you can heal and forgive. Forgiveness brings ultimate freedom. That is why God commanded it. God knows your heart has paid a heavy price by being in a relationship with an abusive person. His desire is to see you free to live the way he created you to live. To forgive your abuser is the grace of freedom. God knew what he was doing when he commanded forgiveness. That is why he took on the part of revenge.

Sometimes it's hard for a person to forgive, because the meaning of forgiveness is misunderstood. So let's get this clear:

- ❧ Forgiveness does *not* mean you forget the wrong committed against you.

- ❧ Forgiveness does *not* mean you are acknowledging that the wrong committed is now okay.

- ❧ Forgiveness does *not* mean you give up the righteous anger you have toward your offender.

- ❧ Forgiveness does *not* mean a renewal of the relationship with your offender.

Jesus said, "Love your enemies, do good to those who hate you, bless those who curse you, pray for those who mistreat you.... Do to others as you would have them do to you. If you love those who love you, what credit is that to you? Even sinners love those who love them. And if you do good to those who are good to you, what credit is that to you? Even sinners do that. And if you lend to those from whom you expect repayment, what credit is that to you? Even sinners lend to sinners, expecting to be repaid in full. But love your enemies, do good to them, and lend to them without expecting to get anything back. Then your reward will be great, and you will be children of the Most High, because he is kind to the ungrateful and wicked. Be merciful, just as your Father is merciful.... Forgive, and you will be forgiven" (Luke 6:27–37).

How do you feel right now about forgiving your abuser?

_____

_____

_____

_____

_____

_____

Do you believe forgiveness is hard? Why?

_____

_____

_____

_____

_____

_____

_____

Do you believe forgiveness will bring you freedom?

_____

_____

_____

_____

What holds you back from forgiving?

_____

_____

_____

_____

_____

_____

_____

A Prayer

Lord, give me peace and rest. My heart and my body are weary. It's been such a long journey, learning to press through the pain and hurt caused from the abuse in my life. Give me strength to trust you, to believe that you do have my back and that you will be my protector, my savior, and my friend.

Lord, please, help me to forgive. In my own strength, I find it impossible to forgive this person. I am so scared of the situation I am in. I need your wisdom to show me what to do and how to begin to find myself again. I need your strength for me to begin this new journey of healing and recovery. I need you to stand beside me every day and to take on the King Sauls of my life.

And when I cannot bear it anymore, Jesus, carry me to safety. Show me the path out. Show me how to find my freedom physically and emotionally.

Amen.

Abuse to Favor

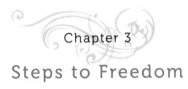

Chapter 3

Steps to Freedom

By Sharon Kay Ball, LPC-MHSP

Physical and emotional abuse are horrific ways to destroy the core of a human being's soul and create fear in the individual. Abuse is trauma in a person's life.

The following steps are suggestions that will get you started on your healing journey. Give yourself permission to follow your heart without condemnation as you heal.

As you begin your healing journey, you will meet grief and its many stages. It is important for you to know that grief is universal, but it is different for each person. Generally the stages of grief do not happen in the same order for everyone. As you move through grief, allow yourself to feel the movement, for where there is movement there is life, and where there is life there is *hope*. You will make it through, only to find yourself stronger. This is the gift of grief. It acknowledges how deep the loss is and then gives you strength to handle the depth of loss. Walk gently with yourself through these stages. Be kind, be still, and breathe. You will be amazed when you embrace your grief and no longer fear it. You will see it as your friend and not your enemy.

Recognizing

Oftentimes, children of physical and emotional abuse will not have anyone to help them process the abuse or the grief that follows. They learn to survive the abusive situation with coping mechanisms that work as a child, but eventually do not work as an adult. These children are more susceptible to "other" abusers in their adult lives. Why? If they haven't processed the abuse as a child and understand their value and have a sense of self, they will minimize or not recognize future abusive acts as abusive.

It is okay to say you were a victim during your childhood. In many ways you're like the victim of a drunk driver. Let's say a drunk driver came toward you across the double yellow lines and hit your car head-on, leaving you paralyzed. Would you say to yourself, *I am not a victim. I could have prevented that drunk driver from crossing the line.* No, of course not. You had nothing to do with the driver choosing to drink and drive. You had everything to do with being the victim in that situation. Remind yourself during this stage that the abuse was not your choice or fault. You were a child. Children do not choose to be abused.

The gift of hope and healing is yours to receive. Only you can accept it and give yourself the option to recover. Remember, you are like an injured person who can choose to go through physical therapy and have a quality of life, or choose not to. Remind yourself that moving from victim to survivor is a process—a vital one to your life. If you truly want to live again, you must choose to be a survivor and disempower the hold that the abuse has had over you. (See "Signs of Abuse" on page 87.)

1. During this time, if you have not left your abuser, you need to begin to make a "safe plan." Do not tell your abuser. Seek help from a local domestic violence shelter and they will help you. (See "Making a Safe Plan" on page 89.)

2. The months after you leave will be a crucial time. You will need to resist the urge of wanting to go back to the familiar. You may feel that trying harder will make a difference, but it doesn't. *Do not go back.* Give yourself a time frame that you and your counselor can work toward. You

may decide to live with a friend or family member for six months to give yourself time to sort things out.

3. Abuse is a cycle. Your abuser will say or do things that make it appear as if he is sorry. However, remind yourself of his behavior patterns. True character change does not happen overnight. An abuser can turn on the charm to try to draw you back in. This is called the honeymoon phase. (See "The Abuse Cycle" on page 92.) Be aware of this tendency, and *do not go back*. Put strict boundaries around yourself.

4. Create a "roundtable" team—a trustworthy team of people, usually three to four, who understand domestic violence and put you and your children's safety first. Rely on these people when you feel weak and vulnerable.

Remembering

This part of your journey will be hard, so it is very important that you be kind and gentle to yourself as you remember the traumas that were done to you. It's not easy to think about past hurts, yet in order to truly heal, you do need to allow those memories to be healed. You have a lifetime. Don't feel as if this has to be an overnight process, but do begin the process.

God gives a child of abuse many coping strategies to get through the hellish times. It is his mercy that allowed you to forget some of these horrific acts or push them aside so that you could try to just be a kid. Those strategies worked during childhood. However, as you entered adulthood, you probably began to see that those strategies no longer worked so well. The strategies of minimization or dismissing the memories became ineffective.

You may find yourself having reoccurring nightmares of the abuse or intrusive thoughts or memories that you cannot control anymore. This is okay. You will be okay. These are signals that deserve to be noticed. They are screaming that this part of your journey needs attention. If you are not quite ready to walk through this with someone safe, when these moments occur, gently allow yourself to sit in the reality of what you went through as a child and ask the Lord to begin the healing process in your heart.

When the abuse took place, whether it was when you were a little girl or an adult, you were unable at the time to stand up for yourself. Take time to write a letter to yourself, describing what you feel you lost when you experienced abuse. This letter is between you and God.

Secrets only carry power when they are kept secret! Speaking with someone about the abuse may be a difficult step; however, it is necessary to squelch the power of secrecy. With secrecy comes shame, and shame will hold you captive. This may take courage, but it could be a very empowering step for you to speak with someone about your story.

Anger

Anger is an emotion that God has given all human beings to let us know when something is wrong. It is a good emotion. During and after your abuse, you felt angry. That was good—very good. Now, though, how you guide your anger allows it to shape-shift and take on action. You have the power to use your anger in a positive way or a negative way. Be very careful not to turn this anger inward—that would allow the abuse to then have power over you again. Explore healthy ways to use your anger—the righteous anger that God gave you to stand up against the wrongs in this world. I recommend the following ways to help you come to terms with your anger:

- Journal about your anger, allowing your thoughts to form on paper. In doing this you might find that the root of your anger is sadness, which may redirect your anger toward mourning your loss. Remind yourself that these thoughts are only thoughts; they do not have power unless put into action. It is when you act upon your anger that you can hurt others. Sometimes just seeing your thoughts written down diffuses what power they might have had. Should you become overwhelmed, talk about these journal entries with your counselor.

- Make a CD or playlist of your favorite inspirational songs, and listen to them when you feel the anger arise.

- Exercise. Take some of the energy that anger brings and run it off!

- Acknowledge your anger; don't stuff it. This anger is looking out for you. Anger is like an alert system warning you that something is wrong. If you ignore the anger, it will sit within you and will surface in ways that you may not like. There is no way to get around anger. Allow yourself to move through it, trusting that God put that emotion in you to alert you to the wrongs in life.

Forgiveness

Forgiveness may be one of the most difficult things you will have to do, understandably. This part of your journey is very private, and for many women, forgiveness happens on a daily basis.

Try writing a letter to your abuser. The letter you write is for you only, so you can see the words that you would say to your abuser. *Do not send it.* Allow your heart to sit with the mixture of emotions that the letter brings up in you.

Ask your counselor if you could speak to your counselor the words that you would like to say to your abuser. If you do this, afterwards explore the feelings this brings up.

Engage God; share with him your reservations and fears about forgiveness.

And remember:

- Forgiveness does *not* mean you forget the wrong committed against you.

- Forgiveness does *not* mean you are acknowledging that the wrong committed is now okay.

- Forgiveness does *not* mean you give up the righteous anger you have toward your offender.

- Forgiveness does *not* mean a renewal of the relationship with your offender.

Your Spiritual Walk

It is important that through your healing and recovery, you take notice of where Jesus is during the process. Is he there beside you, weeping with you? Has he left you? Is he condemning you? Does he take on the emotion of the abuser? During the trauma of abuse, you may have often found yourself seeing Jesus through the grid system of our abuse. This is how Satan would want your spiritual walk to continue. However, through the healing and recovery process, you may begin to notice that your view of Jesus was skewed by the trauma and that he now takes on a healthier role in your life. Journaling will reveal amazing insights into the progression of your spiritual walk during this time.

Making Peace, Moving Forward

The journey of recovery is long and hard. Be very kind and gentle to yourself. There will be days when you feel as if you have gone one step forward and two steps back. You are in charge of your life; therefore, you are responsible for your self-care—no one else.

As healing occurs, you may begin to notice behaviors that you no longer like or that no longer work for you. Be strong and let those go. Acknowledge that they were behaviors and actions that may have kept you feeling safe and in control before, but they are not necessary to live your life anymore. *Let them go.* You do not need them anymore, for you have done the hard process of picking up the shattered pieces and, with God's mercy, putting yourself back together again. So enjoy the freedom to make changes.

Sometimes, the last person you may need to make peace with is not your abuser but yourself. For years you may have considered yourself your worst enemy, critic, and even abuser. It is time to reconcile with yourself. When you can make peace with yourself, you can move forward.

Moving forward may mean you are no longer in crisis mode, that you have found a balance in your life. It is also important to know, however, that there is no end to the healing process. On this side of heaven, your heart will be constantly healing. Only when you are at Jesus' feet will you experience complete and total healing.

Signs of Abuse

Sometimes recognizing abuse is difficult, especially when it is verbal or emotional. The first step to getting out of this cycle is to recognize that your partner's behavior is abusive and that it is not your fault.

Abuse in any form—physical, sexual, verbal, or emotional—slowly erodes your sense of self. In many situations, the victim will sacrifice her views, thoughts, and desires in order to keep herself safe from her partner's behavior. This is the only way she knows how to survive, as she hopes her partner will change. In the end, it is the victim who loses herself to this cycle of abuse. The partner wins his desire of control.

One way to recognize abuse in your relationship is to get back in touch with you! What emotions do you feel when in the presence of your partner? Here are some questions to get you started as you reflect on your relationship:

- Do you fear your partner?

- Do you avoid certain topics so that you do not anger your partner?

- Do you believe you deserve to be yelled at or hit?

- Do you wonder if you are crazy?

- Do you feel emotionally numb or helpless?

- Do you still dream about your future?

- Is your partner's temper unpredictable?

- Has your partner threatened to hurt you, take your children away from you, or kill you?

- Does your partner force you to have sex?

- Does your partner limit your access to friends or money?

- Does your partner blame you for his abusive behaviors?

🕊 Do you feel your partner views you as an object rather than a person?

It is important to understand the abuser. This allows you to place responsibility for the abusive actions *on your partner*, not you.

🕊 An abuser is smart and carefully chooses who, when, and where he is going to abuse.

🕊 An abuser can control himself with other people who make him upset, and he can stop his abusive behavior immediately when doing so works to his advantage.

🕊 An abuser typically acts out in private and will direct his hits and kicks to places on the body that are easily hidden.

Making a Safe Plan

When you believe you are in an abusive relationship, it is important to get help and to come up with a safe plan. An abuser tries to control your life, and when he feels he has lost that control, the abuse often gets worse. So please plan carefully. Here are some ways to get started:

- ❧ Contact your local women's abuse shelter. The shelter staff will be able to get you in touch with a counselor to personalize your safe plan. They will understand what you are going through.

- ❧ Have important numbers nearby for you and your children to make a call for help immediately. Teach your children how to call 911 and make up a code word to teach them if you need them to call the police. Think of four places you can go if you need to leave.

- ❧ Think of how to get out of the house and remove anything that could be used as a weapon. Think of how you will get your children out with you.

- ❧ Think of four people who you can call to help you when you leave. Have their numbers in your cell phone.

🕊 Think of a logical explanation for leaving the house if things get heated: walk your dog, take the trash out, or go to the store.

🕊 Have a hidden safe bag ready. Your safe bag should contain money; extra keys to your car, house, and work; extra clothes; medicines; important papers for you and your children (birth certificates, social security cards, school and medical records, blank checks, credit cards, driver's license, car registration, welfare identification, passports, green cards, work permits, lease or rental agreement, mortgage payment book, unpaid bills, insurance papers, divorce papers, custody orders); address book; pictures; jewelry; things that mean a lot to you; items for your children (toys, blankets, etc.).

🕊 Go over your plan again and again so that it becomes a habit.

The Abuse Cycle

Knowing the abuse cycle will help you identify if you are in an abusive relationship or keep you out of one. This cycle is standard for sexual, physical, emotional, or verbally abusive situations.

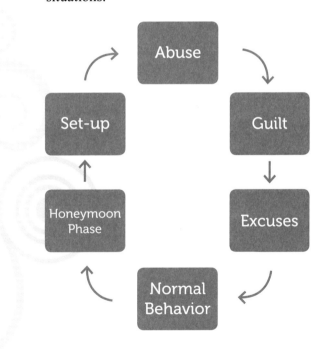

Abuse—The abuser acts out aggressively through rage or humiliating comments. He wants to show you who is in charge. He is a bully in this phase.

Guilt—The abuser goes through a period of guilt. But this is not a feeling of guilt for having hurt you. This guilt is fear of getting caught.

Excuses—The abuser then makes excuses for his behavior rather than taking responsibility.

Normal Behavior—The abuser seeks to regain control over you to keep you in the relationship, and he does so by acting "normal," as if nothing happened.

Honeymoon Phase—This phase gives you (the victim) the energy to hope again that he has changed. But change has typically not occurred.

Set-up—The abuser starts thinking of and planning ways to hurt you again—looking for anything wrong that you have done to set you up and act out the plan. Now, he has "justification" to be aggressive and start the cycle all over again.

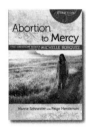
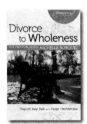

FEAR TO COURAGE

Fear to Courage shows women that they don't have to be a slave to their fears and helps them truly define their fears and develop the courage to move past them. This book shows women that through Christ all things are possible. Paperback, 4.5"x 6.5", 96 pages.

ABANDONMENT TO FORGIVENESS

At some point in every woman's life she has felt a sense of abandonment, for some this feeling is bigger than others. This book teaches women that no matter who has left you, God is always with you. Paperback, 4.5"x 6.5", 96 pages.

DECEIVED TO DELIVERED

She never thought she would cross the line and have an affair, but she did. *Deceived to Delivered* shows women how to strengthen their boundaries and restore their relationships. Paperback, 4.5"x 6.5", 96 pages.